25.65

Date Due

SUPER
SANDCASTLE.
Poetry Power

BUSES
~TO~
BOOKS

Reading, Writing, and Reciting
Poems About School

COMPILED & EDITED BY SUSAN M. FREESE   ILLUSTRATED BY JAN WESTBERG

ABDO
Publishing Company

Published by ABDO Publishing Company, 8000 West 78th Street, Edina, MN 55439. Copyright © 2008 by Abdo Consulting Group, Inc. International copyrights reserved in all countries. No part of this book may be reproduced in any form without written permission from the publisher. Super SandCastle™ is a trademark and logo of ABDO Publishing Company.

Printed in the United States.

Editor: Pam Price
Curriculum Coordinator: Nancy Tuminelly
Cover and Interior Design and Production: Mighty Media

Library of Congress Cataloging-in-Publication Data

Freese, Susan M., 1958-
  Buses to books : reading, writing, and reciting poems about school /
  Susan M. Freese.
    p. cm. -- (Poetry power)
  Includes index.
  ISBN 978-1-60453-002-5
1. Poetry--Authorship--Juvenile literature. 2. Children's poetry, American. 3. Education in literature. I. Title.

PN1059.A9F7425 2008
808.1--dc22

                    2007040257

Super SandCastle™ books are created by a team of professional educators, reading specialists, and content developers around five essential components— phonemic awareness, phonics, vocabulary, text comprehension, and fluency— to assist young readers as they develop reading skills and strategies and increase their general knowledge. All books are written, reviewed, and leveled for guided reading, early intervention reading, and Accelerated Reader® programs for use in shared, guided, and independent reading and writing activities to support a balanced approach to literacy instruction.

About SUPER SANDCASTLE™

Bigger Books for Emerging Readers Grades PreK–3

Created for library, classroom, and at-home use, Super SandCastle™ books support and engage young readers as they develop and build literacy skills and will increase their general knowledge about the world around them. Super SandCastle™ books are part of SandCastle™, the leading preK–3 imprint for emerging and beginning readers. Super SandCastle™ features a larger trim size for more reading fun.

Let Us Know

Super SandCastle™ would like to hear your stories about reading this book. What was your favorite page? Was there something hard that you needed help with? Share the ups and downs of learning to read. We want to hear from you! Send us an e-mail.

sandcastle@abdopublishing.com

Contact us for a complete list of SandCastle™, Super SandCastle™, and other nonfiction and fiction titles from ABDO Publishing Company.
www.abdopublishing.com
8000 West 78th Street Edina, MN 55439
800-800-1312 · 952-831-1632 fax

A Note to Librarians, Teachers, and Parents

The poems in this book are grouped into three sections. "I Can Read" has poems that children can read on their own. "Read With Me" has poems that may require some reading help. "Kids' Corner" has poems written by children.

There are some words in these poems that young readers may not know. Some of these words are in boldface. Their pronunciations and definitions are given in the text. Other words can be looked up in the book's glossary.

When possible, children should first read each poem out loud. That way they will hear all of the sounds and feel all of the rhythms. If it is not possible to read aloud, instruct them to read the poems to themselves so they hear the words in their heads.

The **Poetry Pal** next to each poem explains how the poet uses words and specific styles or techniques to make the reader feel or know something.

The **Speak Up!** sidebar prompts readers to reflect on what they think each poem means and how it relates to them.

Become a Poet! provides ideas and activities to encourage and enhance learning about reading, writing, and reciting poetry.

Contents

 what Is

Let's pretend someone has asked you to write about school. Maybe you hate to do homework or take tests. But you have to follow these rules for writing. First, you can't use very many words. And second, you have to put the words in order so they make a rhyme or a rhythm when you read them.

These are some of the rules for writing poetry. Poetry is different from the writing you do at school and other places, which is called **prose** (PROZE). Here's how!

Poets, the people who write poetry, use fewer words than other kinds of writers. That means they have to pick just the right words to say what they think and feel. The words in poems often are about how things look, feel, smell, taste, and sound. Poets use words to paint pictures for their readers.

4

poetry?

Poets also arrange words in ways to create rhyme and rhythm. You probably know that words that **rhyme** (RIME) sound the same, such as *cat*, *sat*, and *bat*. Rhyming words are fun to say and to hear. A **rhythm** (RIH-thum) is a pattern of sounds. Think about the beat you feel when you clap or march to music. You can feel the same kind of beat when you read a poem. By using rhythm and rhyme, poets make words sound like music.

What else is special about poetry? Because of all the choices poets get to make when they write, no two poems are ever the same. You will see that when you read the poems in this book! And you will find that out when you write your own poems too!

C
S
B at

5

Getting Started

The terms on the next page tell how poets choose words and put them together in special ways. As you read about each term, look at the poem "Brain Power" to see an example.

Brain Power

BY SAM FERNANDEZ

At my desk, I try to study,
But my brain seems kinda muddy.

At the park, I go to play,
And the mud all goes away!

line

A line in a poem is a group of words written across the page. In "Brain Power," the first line is "At my desk, I try to study." Each new line starts below the one before it. There are four lines in this short poem.

stanza
(STAN-zuh)

A stanza is a group of lines in a poem that are usually about the same idea. A stanza is like a paragraph in other kinds of writing. Stanzas are separated by blank lines of space. "Brain Power" has two stanzas.

rhyme
(RIME)

Words that rhyme end with the same sound, such as *dog* and *log* and *fox* and *socks*. In a poem, the last words of the lines often rhyme but not always. In many poems, every pair of lines rhymes or every other line rhymes. In "Brain Power," lines 1 and 2 rhyme and lines 3 and 4 rhyme. Look at the words *study* and *muddy* and *play* and *away*.

rhythm
(RIH-thum)

Even poems that don't rhyme have rhythm, a pattern of sounds or beats. In most poems, some sounds are accented. That means you say them with a little more punch. Read "Brain Power" aloud and listen to which sounds you accent. Clap on these sounds to help you hear and feel them. You probably read line 1 using a pattern like this, "**AT** my **DESK**, I **TRY** to **STU**-dy." To read this line, you accent every other sound, starting with the first one. Line 2 has the same pattern, and so do lines 3 and 4. All the lines in this poem have the same rhythm, or pattern of beats.

I Can Read

Have fun reading the
poems in this section
on your own. If you
have trouble, just ask
someone for help!

9

POETRY PAL

The **speaker** in a poem is the person who's talking. This speaker is talking about the first day of school. Everything seems nice and new, ready for another school year. The speaker feels ready too!

The feeling or mood that a poem creates is called the **tone** (TOHN).

SPEAK UP!

What do you like about the first day of school? What don't you like? Why?

First Day

BY EILEEN SPINELLI

My new teacher smiles.
My pencils are sharp.
My desk is at the window.
Sun spills across my notebook
open to the first page.
First assignment is coming.
Maybe to write a poem.
I am ready.

10

Sharpen, Sharpen, Sharpen

BY KENN NESBITT

Sharpen, sharpen, sharpen.
I crank the handle fast.
Sharpen, sharpen, sharpen.
Until it's sharp at last.

Scribble, scribble, scribble.
Hey wait! It still won't write.
Sharpen, sharpen, sharpen.
I crank with all my might.

Sharpen, sharpen, sharpen.
It must be done, I guess.
Scribble, scribble, dribble.
Oh goodness, what a mess!

Darn it, darn it, darn it.
I guess I'll start again.
Teacher! Teacher! Teacher!
I need another pen.

POETRY PAL

Look at lines 1 and 3 of the first stanza. Both repeat the same word three times. Now look at lines 1 and 3 of the other stanzas. What other words and phrases are repeated? Poets use **repetition** (rep-uh-TIH-shun) to create rhythm. When you say the repeated words, you probably say them quickly and with punch.

SPEAK UP!

What's the little joke at the end of this poem? When did you start to think something was wrong?

POETRY PAL

The speaker in this poem is telling a story about a weird day at school. A poem that tells a story is called a **narrative** (NARE-uh-tiv). The people in the story are called the **characters** (KARE-ick-ters).

The speaker is one of the characters. Why does he or she know this story? The other character is the teacher. The speaker tells us what the teacher did and said to the students.

The talking in a story is called **dialogue** (DY-uh-log). You can tell dialogue by the quotation marks around it.

Nothing
Left to Learn

BY ERIC ODE

It all occurred on March the third,
 a Tuesday afternoon.
Our teacher shook her head and said,
"It may as well be June.

"Although it's clear we will be here
 for many months to go,
 I've nothing left to teach you
 that you don't already know.

"So stack your pencil cases,
 and we'll place them in a drawer.
Your books go in a closet.
We don't need them anymore.

12

"Then do your best to scrub your desk
and straighten up your rows."
She bit her lip and sniffed a bit,
and then she blew her nose.

"It's such a shame." My teacher sighed
and gave my desk a rinse.
Those were the final words we heard.
She hasn't spoken since.

And now each day we sit and wait.
The minutes slowly turn,
with sixteen weeks till school is out
but nothing left to learn.

13

SPEAK UP!

An old saying tells us to be
careful what we wish for. That
could be the **moral** (MORE-ull),
or lesson, taught by this story. Think
about what life would be like if you
knew everything. Would anything be
interesting or fun anymore?

English Is a Pain!
(Pane?)

BY SHIRLEE CURLEE BINGHAM

Rain, reign, rein,
English is a pain.
Although the words
sound just alike,
the spelling's not the same!

Bee, be, B,
I'd rather climb a tree,
than learn to spell
the same old word,
not just one way, but three!

14

to
two
too
2

sight site cite

there
their
they're

Sight, site, cite,
I try with all my might.
No matter which
I finally choose,
it's not the one that's right!

There, their, they're,
enough to make you swear.
Too many ways
to write one sound,
I just don't think it's fair!

To, two, too,
so what's a kid to do?
I think I'll go
to live on Mars,
and leave this mess with ewe!
(you?)

SPEAK UP!

People who are learning English often have trouble with homonyms. What do you think would be hard about learning another language? Do you know how to speak more than one language? If not, would you like to?

15

Science Test

BY DARREN SARDELLI

I think I failed my science test,
My stomach's tied in knots.
My ears are clogged, my nose is stuffed,
I'm seeing purple spots.
I cannot feel my toes or feet,
My arms are very weak.
My back is in tremendous pain.
It's difficult to speak.
I should have been excused today,
but mom said I looked fine.
I think my fever should have been
a GIANT warning sign!
I cannot breathe! I'm turning blue!
There's something on my chest...
What's that you say?
I got an A!
I knew I passed this test!

The Bus

BY ROBERT POTTLE

Sixty kids and one adult,
you gotta love those odds.
The perfect place for pulling pranks
and throwing paper wads.
Hank is standing on his head.
Billy's playing ball.
Peter wet his pants again.
Tasha pushes Paul.
Steven steals. Kevin cries.
Millicent is missing.
Katie punched her cousin Keith.
Ben and Jen are kissing.
Me, I'm taking lots of notes
on public transportation.
I think the bus provides me with
the finest education.

17

POETRY PAL

Line 3 says the bus is "The perfect place for pulling pranks." Do you hear all the *p* sounds in that line? Repeating the same sound at the beginnings of words is called **alliteration** (uh-lit-ur-AY-shun).

Find places where kids' names and actions both start with the same sound, such as *Kevin cries*.

SPEAK UP!

The speaker is learning a lot by riding the bus! What can you learn from seeing what others do wrong?

Read With Me

18

Enjoy reading these poems with someone who can help you with the harder words and ideas. Poetry is more fun when you understand what you are reading!

Michael O'Toole

BY PHIL BOLSTA

Michael O'Toole hated going to school,
He wanted to stay home and play.
So he lied to his dad and said he felt bad
And stayed home from school one day.

The very next day he decided to say
That his stomach felt a bit queasy.
He groaned and he winced 'til his dad was convinced,
And he said to himself, "This is easy!"

At the end of the week, his dad kissed his cheek,
And said, "Son, you've missed too much school."
"But still I feel funny, and my nose is all runny,"
Said the mischievous Michael O'Toole.

20

Each day he'd complain of a new ache or pain,
But his doctor could find nothing wrong.
He said it was best to let Michael rest,
Until he felt healthy and strong.

Michael O'Toole never did get to school,
So he never learned how to write—
Or to read or to spell or do anything well,
Which is sad, for he's really quite bright.

And now that he's grown, he sits home alone
'Cause there's nothing he knows how to do.
Don't be a fool and stay home from school,
Or the same thing could happen to you!

SPEAK UP!

This narrative poem tells the sad story of a boy who lies to stay home from school. What happens to him? What's the moral, or lesson, of the story?

Homework, I Love You

BY KENN NESBITT

Homework, I love you. I think that you're great.
It's wonderful fun when you keep me up late.
I think you're the best when I'm totally stressed,
preparing and cramming all night for a test.

Homework, I love you. What more can I say?
I love to do hundreds of problems each day.
You boggle my mind and you make me go blind,
but still I'm ecstatic that you were assigned.

Homework, I love you. I tell you, it's true.
There's nothing more fun or exciting to do.
You're never a chore, for it's you I adore.
I wish that our teacher would hand you out more.

Homework, I love you. You thrill me inside.
I'm filled with emotions. I'm fit to be tied.
I cannot complain when you frazzle my brain.
Of course, that's because I'm completely insane.

22

History

BY MYRA COHN LIVINGSTON

And I'm thinking how to get out
Of this stuffy room
With its big blackboards.

And I'm trying not to listen
In this boring room
To the way things *were*.

And I'm thinking about later,
Running from the room
Back into the world,

And what the guys will say when
I'm up to bat and hit
A big fat home run.

POETRY PAL

Compared with the other poems in this book, what's different about this one? What's missing?

The lines in this poem don't have a steady rhythm, or pattern of beats. And none of the lines rhyme! This kind of poem is called **free verse**. It sounds a lot like how people talk.

SPEAK UP!

What kinds of things do you think about when you're bored?

Like the last poem, this one is about letting your mind wander during school. Sally is thinking about riding her horse, crossing rivers and streams and racing across deserts and meadows and valleys. You can probably see her in your mind!

This poem paints pictures with words, creating **imagery** (IM-udge-ree).

SPEAK UP!

Draw a picture of Sally riding her horse in one of the places described in the poem.

Sally's Not at School Today

BY ERIC ODE

Sally's not at school today although she's at her desk.
She's sitting prim and proper and looks rather picturesque.
She seems to be attentive with her hair tied up in tails,
but in her head she's on her horse, and riding on the trails.

That horse is chasing rivers and is drinking from a pool,
and Sally's in the saddle and a hundred miles from school.
They're racing through the desert, and they're crossing mountain streams
and running through the meadows and the valleys of her dreams.

Her teacher thinks she sees her seated sweetly in her chair,
but no one seems to recognize that Sally isn't there.
She's speeding through a canyon like a train along the rails.
Sally's not at school today. She's riding on the trails.

24

You Can Dance with a Book

BY EILEEN SPINELLI

You can dance with a book.
Take a chance with a book.
Have a don't-want-to-finish
romance with a book.

You can learn from a book.
Take a turn with a book.
And discover—surprise!—
that you yearn for a book.

You can cry with a book.
Bake a pie with a book.
And when sleep doesn't come—
lullaby with a book.

You can lend a good book.
And pretend with a book.
Best of all—
you can make a dear friend
of a book.

25

POETRY PAL

Did you know you could do so many things with a book? Count how many things are listed. A poem that has a list is called a **catalog** (CAT-uh-log) **poem**.

Also count how many times the word *book* is used. This poem makes good use of repetition!

SPEAK UP!

The poem says a book can become "a dear friend." What's your favorite book? Why?

Kids' Corner

This poem is a **metaphor** (METT-uh-for), which tells about one thing by describing something else. In this metaphor, a student talks about her desk like it's a monster.

Pick something from your classroom, school building, or playground. What does it make you think of? Maybe a dark closet makes you think of a cave. Maybe something on the playground seems like a spaceship. Write three lines that tell about the one thing by describing the other thing.

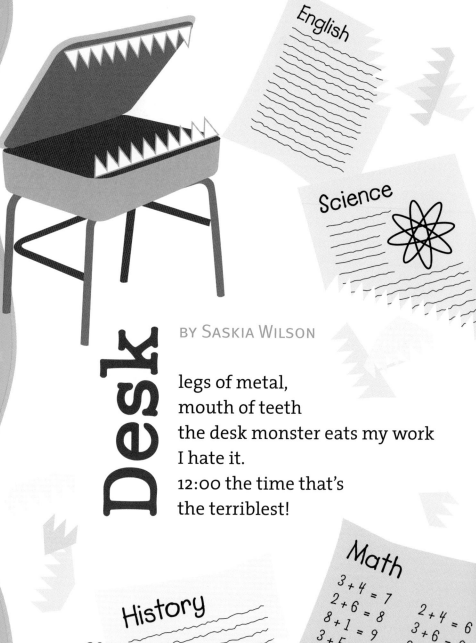

English

Science

Desk

BY SASKIA WILSON

legs of metal,
mouth of teeth
the desk monster eats my work
I hate it.
12:00 the time that's
the terriblest!

Math

3 + 4 = 7
2 + 6 = 8
8 + 1 = 9
3 + 5 = 8
6 + 1 = 7
4 + 1 = 5

2 + 4 = 6
3 + 6 = 9
2 + 2 = 4
3 + 3 = 4

History

26

Books

BY ELLA KAPLAN

books
books
look in
books
look
in
the
book
now
see
things
read
things
and
be
things

27

POETRY PAL

Like the poem "Dance with a Book," this poem lists things to do with books. Write your own **list,** or **catalog poem** about your favorite or least favorite subject in school.

If you write about your favorite subject, list words that tell what you like about it. If you write about your least favorite subject, list words that tell what you don't like. You could also list the things you do or use in this subject. Put one word or idea on each line in your poem.

Become a Poet!

Here are some activities to help you write your own poems.

Keep a Journal

Many writers keep a journal, which is a book of ideas, thoughts, and drawings. Start your own journal in an empty notebook. Write down ideas for your own poems. Write down things that happen, what you like and don't like. Keep your journal with you so you can use it often.

Learn New Words

In the back of your journal, make a list of new words you learn. Start with the words you learned while reading the poems in this book. Write down each word and what it means. Then write each word in a sentence to make sure you know how to use it. Also write down how to say it if you think you won't remember.

Make a Picture

Draw or paint a picture about one of the poems in this book. Maybe pick one of the poems that has many words about colors and other things you can see. Share both the poem and the picture with someone.

Write a Story

Choose one of the poems in this book and write a story from it. Your story can be about what's happening in the poem or who's in the poem. Write using your own words, not the words from the poem.

Have a Poetry Reading

With a few friends or family members, put on a show where everyone has a turn to read a poem out loud. When people aren't reading, they should be in the audience. Practice using correct rhythm and rhyme beforehand. Also make sure you know all the words. Try reciting the poem from memory, if you can.

Find More Poems

What's your favorite poem in this book? Who wrote it? Use the Internet and books in your library to find another poem by this poet. Read the new poem several times. Then read your favorite poem again. How are the two poems alike? How are they different? Which poem do you like best now? Write about the poems in your journal.

Learn About Poets

Use the Internet or books in your library to learn about famous poets. Start with Kenn Nesbitt, who writes a lot of children's poems. Where is he from? What poems has he written? Read four poems by Kenn Nesbitt and pick your favorite. Write down in your journal why you like this poem the best.

Make a Recording

Record yourself reading one of the poems from this book out loud. Practice so you can read the poem with the correct rhythm and rhyme. Ask your parent or teacher for help, if you need it. Record other poems later to make a set of your favorite poems.

Glossary

attentive – listening or watching carefully.

convince – to make someone believe or do something.

cram – to study a lot at the last minute.

ecstatic – being really happy.

insane – crazy and unable to think clearly.

mischievous – tending to behave in a way that causes trouble or irritation to others.

picturesque – having a pleasing appearance.

queasy – feeling sick in the stomach.

recognize – to notice or realize.

tremendous – very large in size, amount, or power.

wince – to shrink back or flinch from pain or fear.

yearn – to want very much.

permissions

Index